AN HOMAGE TO JEROME

Valery Larbaud

AN HOMAGE TO JEROME
Patron Saint of Translators

Translated from the French
and with a preface by
Jean-Paul de Chezet

THE MARLBORO PRESS

T M P

MARLBORO, VERMONT
1984

Originally published as "Le Patron des Traducteurs," in SOUS L'INVOCATION DE SAINT JEROME. © Editions Gallimard, 1946.

Cover illustration: *Saint Jerome,* by an unknown artist, Veneto-Byzantine School, late 14th Century. The David and Alfred Smart Gallery, The University of Chicago, Chicago, Illinois; Gift of the Samuel H. Kress Foundation, 1973.41.

Manufactured in the United States of America.

Library of Congress Catalog Card Number 83-63447

ISBN 0-910395-09-8

PREFACE

Valery Larbaud always had the opportunity to travel as he pleased for he had the leisure and the mobility that come with wealth. He was the heir to the Vichy Saint-Yorre springs and, like his best-known fictional character, A. O. Barnabooth, a *riche amateur.* So, between the ages of eighteen and fifty-four, Larbaud travelled wherever his fancy led. Yet, and though he had his hero Barnabooth—in many ways his alter ego—hail from South America and become a naturalized citizen of the State of New York, Larbaud never came to the United States. One might wonder why, for he was strongly attracted to American letters and had many friends here, through whose help he procured the complete works of Hawthorne, Thoreau and Whitman (whose writings he translated in part) and T. S. Eliot, among others. As a matter of fact, it seems that as a young man Larbaud entertained the idea of a trip to the United States as a kind of pilgrimage to the graves of Whitman and Poe. At least so says an American acquaintance of his, who reports that during a conversation he had with him, Larbaud, by then incapacitated and no longer able to travel, in a halting and wistful voice named a few of the places he wished he had visited in America.[1]

Several possible explanations for his failure to carry out such a project come to mind. First, his generally unpredictable health, precarious from birth. Second, the fact that he seems to have been happiest on terra firma: he rarely ventured upon the seas, apart from several Channel crossings and an occasional Mediterranean cruise; and never boarded an airplane. He was content to crisscross Europe, which he explored mostly by train, starting at the age of eighteen when he jour-

---

1. See V. Vincent Milligan, "Hommage à Valery Larbaud" in *La Nouvelle Revue Française,* September, 1957, p. 571.

neyed all the way to Constantinople via Saint Petersburg and Moscow. The best explanation probably lies with the order of his priorities: he loved to follow the sun, ordinarily heading south—again and again to Italy and Spain, once to Portugal—, making one exception in favor of London and the southern English countryside. An aesthete and a humanist, fluent in Greek and Latin as well as Spanish and Italian, he felt an irresistible attraction for Greco-Roman civilization. Never tiring for long of the warm sun and gentle breezes of peaceful Alicante and Tuscany, he simply must have felt no imperious desire to cross the Atlantic and know the frantic pace of our cities.

Yet Larbaud, though born in provincial Vichy in 1881, was soon exposed to life in a busy metropolis when his mother took him to Paris after his septuagenarian father died in 1889. He loved Paris and always kept an apartment there for a home base. Vichy, which he associated with his domineering mother, he never liked, much preferring the quiet of his aunt's nearby country estate of Valbois. Indeed, Paris is where he spent the best three years of his youth—perhaps the best three years of his life—as a boarder in a fashionable private *collège* that catered in particular to the capital's colony of South American diplomats and wealthy exiles. The remembrance of those enchanted years inspired his best-known novel, *Fermina Marquez* (1911), the subtle, tender and ever-so-chaste evocation of his *amours enfantines.*

Larbaud very early demonstrated a remarkable gift for languages and writing, and finished his *licence-ès-lettres* while travelling almost constantly, first when taken in tow by his mother, a devotee of fashionable spas, then on his own or in the company of friends, soon all female. Thus did he spend the first thirty-three years of his life, moving from one villa, hotel or pension to the next, writing and rewriting short works of fiction and literary essays or making translations of English, American, Spanish, Portuguese and Italian authors, rarely staying more than three months at a time in any one place. A most restless existence for a fundamentally retiring sort of man. In 1922 he married Maria-Angela Nebbia, of Genoa, who remained his devoted companion until his death in Paris in 1957.

When, in 1935, he was felled by a stroke that left him partially paralyzed and with his speech permanently impaired, Larbaud had been working on *Sous l'invocation de Saint Jérôme,* a collection of essays on criticism and translation, preceded by an homage to the author of the Vulgate. There is disagreement among his biographers over the importance of religion in his life in general and with respect to St Jerome in particular. Whether in his own journal or in the other he kept, vicariously, on Barnabooth's behalf, Larbaud was always quite secretive about his private life, sentimental or spiritual. Thus he did not tell even his best friends, let alone his Protestant mother, of his conversion to Catholicism in 1910. To what extent, then, was his faith the basis of his devotion to Jerome? It is more likely that this affinity had its origins elsewhere: in the traits of character or, at least, the inclinations the two men shared. Both were great travelers, and openly disliked their native towns. Both were great collectors of books, with Larbaud, in addition, collecting toy soldiers—one suspects for their brightly colored uniforms rather than for their martial significance, Larbaud being of an internationalist disposition—as well as miniature flags, again because of their vivid hues; one of his volumes of essays even bears the title *Jaune Bleu Blanc,* those simply being the colors of his personal ensign. Both men had inquiring minds and a vast store of knowledge. At the time Jerome acceded to Pope Damasus' request that he become his personal secretary, and was put in charge of producing a new version of the Latin Bible, he was considered one of Christendom's most learned sages. Let us not forget that, thanks notably to Erasmus' and Larbaud's accolades, he came to be revered as the patron saint of humanists as well as of translators. For his part, Larbaud, house-ridden during the last twenty-two years of his life, kept mentally active, constantly revising his works and, for relaxation, listening to Europe's many radio stations for hours, or reading the *Petit Larousse Illustré*. Finally, both lived in Italy for a significant part of their lives: Jerome first as an adolescent, later as an aspiring prelate; Larbaud as a lover of the arts and of gracious living, engaged in repeated pilgrimages, whether spiritual or aesthetic, to the Eternal City. But there, perhaps, the similarities with Jerome end, for Larbaud was no ascetic and no censor, no enemy of creature comforts and no Cato; and if he shared his mentor's apparent attraction for children and women, his interest in love clearly went beyond the spiritual and the sacred. Obviously, Larbaud and Jerome were the products of vastly different times; yet the passage of some fifteen centuries does not seem to have broken the continuity between the master and the disciple, in terms of their common humanity and culture. The feeling of spiritual kinship that permeates Larbaud's evocation of Jerome is but one of the many charms of the account he left us of his Roman peregrinations.

—Jean-Paul de Chezet

AN HOMAGE TO JEROME

Why should we not keep by us
the portraits of great men
for the sake of our inspiration,
and celebrate their birthdays?

Seneca

THE IDEA of an essay titled *On the Eminent Dignity of Translators Within the Republic of Letters* seems, off-

hand, a good one. Right away one thinks of the parallel—apt to be pursued with varying degrees of success—that could be drawn with Bossuet's sermon "On the Eminent Dignity of the Poor Within the Church." One can imagine the following development:

The Translator is unrecognized; he sits in the last row; he survives on hand-outs; he consents to perform the most insignificant functions, to perform in the humblest, the most modest roles. "To serve" is his motto, and for himself he asks nothing, seeking no other glory than being faithful to the masters he has chosen for himself, faithful down to the annihilation of his own intellectual personality. To ignore him, to deny him any consideration, to mention his name, most often, merely in order to accuse him—and frequently without any proof—of having betrayed those whom he wished to interpret, and to look down upon him even when his work pleases us . . . is to scorn the most precious qualities and the rarest virtues: self-abnegation, patience, charity itself, a scrupulous honesty, intelligence, finesse, a vast knowledge, a rich and ready memory—virtues and qualities some of which may be missing in the best minds, but which are never present in mediocre ones.

We must therefore respect and even publicly honor in the able and conscientious Translator those traces of the perfections we worship in that which we consider the very highest; therefore, along with his name and his merits, we must praise the powers of the intelligible world which he gloriously and modestly makes accessible to us. . . .

Such could be the substance and plan of that literary sermon, lofted upon wings of platonic oratory, but which, as it sought rare altitudes, would lose sight of an essential aspect of its subject, as well as of a most important argument in favor of its thesis: we are referring to the importance of the role played by translators in intellectual history, in short their usefulness.

I I

IT is precisely this consideration that induced us to reject the title which our imagination, proud of its find, brought back from some mysterious journey in the direction of Meaux;[1] and to decide instead to stick to a resolution made long ago, namely, to gather all our thoughts touching translators, the art of translation, as well as all of the literary, moral, philological and technical questions relating to that art, and to place them *Under the Protection of St Jerome,*[2] St Jerome, father of the Latin Bible, author of a large part of the Vulgate, hence considered the patron—in the fullest sense of the word—of translators: in this world, their model; in the next, their protector.

This title, which announces and covers the whole subject, seems to us as effective an appeal to the reader's curiosity as that other which recalls and seems to parody the title of the famous sermon. Moreover, this howsoever slight touch of irony with respect to so grave a subject as Poverty, and in connection with so interesting a subject as Translation, is out of place and in our view constitutes one more reason for preferring the old title to the new.

1. Bossuet (1627–1704) is frequently referred to as "l'évêque" or "l'aigle" of Meaux, now just a small town outside of Paris. (Tr. note.)
2. *Sous l'invocation de Saint Jérôme* is the title of the volume that opens with the present essay. (Tr. note.)

THIS being said, we hardly need add that we intend nothing disrespectful at all in placing this text of ours under the aegis of one of the most illustrious doctors of the Roman Church—"Doctor Doctorum, Doctor Maximus"—and one of the foremost Christian saints; and no one reading these pages—no, not even the devoted servants of Jerome's glory, his hermits of St Onofrio[1] on the Janiculum[2]—will be moved to remind us of the saying: *Scherza coi fanti, lascia stare i Santi.*[3]

Indeed, nothing seems to us more impertinent, more uncivilized, than the sentimental and mocking tone, the attitude of jeering condescension, that some writers have assumed when dealing with the works, the personality and the ideas of the great figures of Christian classical literature. Let a pagan author relate Vespasian's[4] miracles in Egypt, or the wondrous events that coincided with the final upheavals that beset the Roman Empire, and they readily absolve him, invoking the ignorance of his times and the prejudices of his nation; but when a Christian author is involved, such displays of credulity become those unforgivable mistakes that disqualify him, that discredit even the most substantial and strongest part of his works. In these, they see nothing but error, touching naiveté, and the rantings of grown-up children who believe in fairy-tales. But did these very same moderns ever ask themselves what sort of a figure they would cut a few centuries hence, with

1. A monastic order devoted jointly to St Jerome and St Onofrio, whose representations in Christian art are often quite similar. (Tr. note.)
2. One of Rome's seven hills. (Tr. note.)
3. "Mock all and sundry, but let the saints be." (Tr. note.)
4. The Roman Emperor (9–79 A.D.) whose accomplishments were in fact deemed miraculous by a portion of his subjects. (Tr. note.)

their "modern ideas," their "insights," the concessions they have made to the prejudices of their own time, and to the fashions, the modes of thought, the spirit of their caste and country? And, for instance, what their bourgeois philanthropy would look like when compared to Jerome's Christian charity? If they had asked themselves those questions, they would probably have paid St Jerome the same respectful attention they unquestioningly grant the best pagan writers who preceded the fall of Rome.

I V

LIKE them, and to the same extent, St Jerome could be one of the companions, one of the guides to our most intimate and most reflective life; an intellectual patron, an example and exhortation, a rich protector of our poverty, whose vast and varied achievement would be for us, in the dimension of time, what any of those great ancient European cities to which we repeatedly return and never grow tired of visiting and exploring, is in space: "Hieronymopolis," the Hieronymian City. For his works are not historical or moral or aesthetic curiosities, they are quick with life and human warmth; the energy they discharge wins an instantaneous response from us; and let our eyes come to rest upon some of his *Prefaces* to the various Books of the Vulgate or upon some of his *Letters,* and the great thinker, writer, and artist stands out at once.

Why, then, do we not consult him more often, we who willingly read his most famous contemporaries or colleagues in the history of Christian Latin literature, St Augustine in particular but Lactantius and St Cyprian as well, even venturing sometimes into Tertullian's, Arnobius' and St Ambrose's domains, while waiting, in libraries, for books to come from the stacks? Is it because excessive and sometimes clumsy or indiscreet publicity has surrounded his name and person (along with a whole train of foolish medieval legends to which his own writings constantly give the lie) and because we are suspicious, as the more discriminating reader is suspicious of and shuns those authors that are launched with great fanfare? But about this there is nothing Jerome can do. To be sure, he yearned, as every true writer must yearn, for literary immortality. Indeed, conscious of his worth, he promised himself, in precise and grand terms, that he would gain it: at the end of St Paula's Epitaph (*Letter CVIII,* addressed to Julia Eustochium) and again at the end of Blaesilla's Epitaph (*Letter XXXIX,* to St Paula): "Wherever the monuments of Latin literature (*sermonis nostri monumento*) will endure, Blaesilla will travel with my writings. The virgins, the widows, the monks, the priests, they will read her, as she lives, fixed in my thought. The memory of her, everlasting, will compensate for the brevity of her life. She who lives in Heaven with Christ will also live upon the lips of men. This generation will pass, and others will succeed it, who will judge without love or hatred. Her name will be placed between those of Paula and Eustochium. In my books she will never die. Forever will she hear me speaking of her with her sister, with her mother." But, living as he did upon the morrow of Christianity's victory, he certainly did not foresee the glorious posthumous life in store for the saintly Writers, nor the more than imperial apotheosis in deference to which, century after century, his name was engraved above the entrance of temples, attracting there the attention and the curiosity of innumerable and ever-renewed crowds—who did not read him, and never will.... "Preferential treatment, an injustice, exaggerated and undeserved advertisement, all the while pagan and lay authors and, among the Christians, even Origen and Tertullian...." For sure; but had the official pagan religion won out, had the hierarchy devised by

Maximian and reestablished by Julian—the competition, hastily and belatedly organized but with pretty strong arguments on its side—prevailed, today would we not see, next to the temples and basilicas devoted to the deified emperors, public monuments (porticoes, praying stations, "churches") dedicated to the heroes of pagan thought—deified too, and with even more reason? Consider the philosophic sects, with their organization and their secular traditions, the teachings of Plotinus and of Porphyry, and the importance they ascribe to the term *hierophant:* do they not reveal an incipient flowering of religions and the first outlines of a universal church? And cannot our imagination thence lead us through towns—our own towns—where temples rise in dedication to Pythagoras, Zeno, Socrates, or where we read the names of Plato, Epictetus, Ammonius Saccas . . . and "St Philo," "St Seneca the Philosopher," "St Virgil Poet" . . . with each century, each generation adding some new name to this Pantheon, down to our own day when we find in the monuments built to the memory of our dead scientists and artists, spontaneous, independent, sporadic manifestations of a religion featuring unknown gods and the cult of their hierophants? But at a given moment, that which was "in the air" materialized and found form and expression. Independently of the actual spreading of the Word and the propagation of Martyrdom, literati, philosophers, writers, following St Paul—the Apologists like that Quadratus "a disciple of the Apostles and Pontiff of the Church of Athens" under the reign of Hadrian—had composed for the use of the emperors and of the intellectual elite a series of treatises and literary works in favor of "our religion"; and this is why at the critical moment, where the body lay the eagles assembled, and a great majority of the intelligentsia opted against the Eleusinian mysteries and for the mystery of the Incarnation.

V

TODAY as in evangelical times, Jesus Christ has his abode in the houses of his friends. There, God is at home just as, in kingdoms, the king's castle is wherever he enters. In the course of centuries, the faithful have raised beautiful houses where Jerome could receive King Jesus; and he has more of them than the most flourishing States have embassies, legations and consulates in cities all over the five continents. But we will not be able to find any trace of him at the spot where he was born: Stridon perished before he did, trampled under by the barbarian invaders: we do not even know where Stridon was. It seems he lived there only briefly, did not like the place, and spoke of it the way many another young man has spoken of his home town, when he heard some inner voice tell him that "Troy is not big enough for you." Of Stridon he wrote: "A country of rustics . . . their belly is their god . . . the richest among them are deemed the most worthy of respect"—so felt Jerome (and so felt Leopardi on the subject of Recanati, and Stendhal on that of Grenoble). "Wo lag Stridon?" wonders a bishop of the old Austro-Hungarian Empire. At Grahovo, perhaps; but in Jerome's works for a certainty, as he is the only one to mention the place. It has been situated on the confines of Pannonia and Dalmatia, but on Italian soil; north-east of the Adriatic; on the threshold of a still half-barbaric Middle-Europe, the large town thereabouts being Aquileia. According to the legend built around him, and because of the vagueness of that location, he is commonly believed to be a native of Dalmatia or Illyria, so that, centuries later, the Dalmatians, the Southern Slavs, the Slavonians[1] congregate round his name. In Bethlehem where he spent the second half of his life—thirty-

1. Better known under their Italian name: Schiavoni. (Tr. note.)

five years—and where he died, he was on home ground all right, but in a foreign land, at the head of a Latin community of monks living in a country that spoke another tongue. But it is in the Catholic capital, in Cosmopolis itself, that we shall feel closest to his memory. "Of me, a Roman, they dare ask . . ." and "to me who received the vestment of Christ in the city of Rome. . . ." He returned to it posthumously: Rome reclaimed him from Bethlehem-Ephrata, and his remains were interred under the relic of the Manger, in the chapel of the Holy Sacrament within Liberius' Basilica, one of the most richly adorned, most luxurious buildings in the world. In the basilica founded by the pope who baptized him. In Rome where he spent the most troubled and the most important years of his adolescence as well as the most prosperous of his maturity, according to general opinion. The Rome of his "wayward youth," the Rome of his "cardinalate," when he was Pope Damasus' secretary, a virgin, and a poet. This is the time when as head of a half religious, half literary school he founded a spiritual family comprising an elite of the city's Christians and its most pious, virtuous and learned ladies, princesses whose names were the talk of the town in the days of the Republic and of the Empire, and whose ancestors go beyond Homer's heroes all the way back to the Gods.[1] Some of them accompanied him to, or joined him in, Bethlehem, in his glorious exile. What his renown and his influence were during the years in Rome that followed his return from Chalcis and Constantinople can be gauged by his enemies' venom, treacherousness, and furious fits of envy that eventually drove him back into the desert. He never returned alive to Rome, but he remained present there thanks to his fame; as long as he lived, his influence never waned. Back from Bethlehem his thought continued to come along with his writings, which indeed were penned for Rome, were read in Rome and commented there: it was for

1. St Paula was a descendant of Aemilius Paullus and of Agamemnon.

"Roman ears"—Rome's own, first, and then the ears of all the Latin West—that he elaborated his monumental work as translator and exegete. "Babylon!"—yet despite the epithet he hurls at her as he leaves, he remains Jerome the Roman. (His is already the era during which "Roman" and "Christian" and shortly "Catholic" become the synonyms they will be in a famous passage by Paulus Orosius.) In effect, that "Babylon!" of his is not the angry cry of a defeated man, but the admonishment of a master of contemporary thought in the Western, Roman, Christian world. Rome became "Babylon" because the Hieronymite ideal of the "perfect life" was rejected by many who were incapable of perceiving its beauty and of confronting its stringencies; an ideal maligned by a rabble of intriguing clerics, the first and especially greedy exploiters of Christianity's triumph, the very ones he describes with a wealth of details and a satiric force which make Molière and even Voltaire seem timid . . . and decent. "Babylon" because only a rare few, and not Rome as a whole, had understood his doctrine and followed his example. It is the expression of a state of mind characteristic of many other thinkers who have run into indifference, stupidity or envy (*Letter XLV,* to Asella, proves, and the medieval legend—the at any rate unlikely legend—of Jerome arrayed as a woman[1] indicates, the role played by envy in this matter) and who, prompted by the desire for a more complete independence and made uncomfortable by their own celebrity, have voluntarily given up the herd-like existence in the big

1. In the *Golden Legend,* under September 30th: "One day, upon awakening, he found on his bed a woman's dress, placed there by people who bore him ill. Thinking it was his own garment (the scholar's absentmindedness!) he put it on and went to church, which permitted people to say that he had had a woman in his bed. Whereupon, unwilling to be exposed to further foolishness, he left Rome. . . ." (Jacques de Voragine, as translated by Teodor Von Wysewa.) We have here the aftermath of the calumnies which circulated in Rome around the years 384–85, and in which the name of Jerome was linked with that of his noble lady-friends and devotees from the Aventine Hill.

city, as did, closer to us in time, Descartes, Bayle, Voltaire, Nietzsche, Tolstoy; and even, if some comparison were possible between men of such inimical or different minds, Jerome's withdrawal to Bethlehem[1] would best be likened to Tolstoy's retirement at Yasnaya Polyana. Nevertheless, Rome remained for him the vital center, the hub of the world and, in particular, "the pristine spring of the Faith," the city forever destined to be the "eternal" one. Rome reborn, founded a second time upon the relics of the Apostles, and whose name means "strength" in Greek, "sublimity" in Hebrew, and which when read in reverse becomes the name of the sacred Love[2] that binds the faithful to one another, and man to God. In Rome, the monk without a family, a homeland, or any earthly ties, had found his home. And through his last *Letters* we see that the fall of the Eternal City was for him a more telling blow than any of the most violent and slanderous attacks from his enemies. (In truth, he must have become inured to those attacks, old hand that he was in the art of polemics, forever slandered, forever replying in kind.)

1. G. Bardy, in his recent manual on Christian Latin literature goes so far as to say that Bethlehem had become "in a way the intellectual center of the Church" because Jerome had chosen to live there.
2. An anagram of the Latin *Amor*. (Tr. note.)

BUT the house of Jerome the Roman, where shall we find it in Rome if we want some day to thank his memory for the gifts he bestowed on us and, once near him, in his home, to think of who he was, of what he is for us, and to ask, perhaps, that by his prayers he preserve us from sloth, discouragement, wrong renderings, and the pernicious advice of bilingual dictionaries?

In Santa Maria Maggiore his body is bathed in the radiance emanating from the Manger, in the splendor of the Americas' gold, and among the dazzling white marbles and snows of Our Lady of the Snows.

In St Onofrio, on the Janiculum, despite the monastery occupied by his hermits nearby and the frescoes of Domenichino, we would not feel quite in his home, but rather in that of Onofrio or of Tasso who is buried there. To be sure, in the vicinity of the Farnese Palace there exists a St Jerome Doctor or a St Jerome of Charity; but for most Romans, St Jerome's church is San Girolamo degli Schiavoni.

AND SO, the next time we are in Rome, we shall pay a visit to the Patron Saint of Translators in his St Jerome of the Slavonians. To get to that church, we shall avoid the Via Tomacelli—too wide, noisy, and asphalted—even though it would take us there directly from the Corso. Instead, we shall go through a zone of grandeur and silence: around the Borghese Palace and to its very end: the keyboard of the harpsichord, which faces the quay on the Tiber. From there it is to the right, and we still have to cross the Via Tomacelli after the Via Arancio. The unpleasantness is soon past: once across, we are already within the district of Augustus' Mausoleum and in front of Jerome's abode.

In the late afternoon of this Roman spring day and through the dark foliage of the holm oaks, we have watched the sky over the city grow a deeper and deeper blue—cerulean, celestial Palestine. Let us touch one of the panels of the large door: it is warm from the sun that has been shining on it for hours on end. At the top, under the papal tiara, Sixtus the Fifth's coat of arms appears; Sixtus, with whose name every edition of the Vulgate opens. He was the patron of St Jerome of the Slavonians when he was elected pope; a coincidence that gives one pause: from Heaven the Translator designates his Publisher. . . . But let us go in.

No crowds about. The peaceful silence and light of a library—*caelestis Bibliothecae cultor*[1]—; dark frescoes, rich and restful. A quiet, royal, monastic opulence, with its marbles, its panelling. San Rocco, a few steps away in the Via Ripetta, receives many more visitors and it has electrically-lit glass flowers and an Our Lady of Lourdes chapel which resembles a big drained-out aquarium, with a Virgin Mary and a St Bernadette that look like paper cut-outs pasted on cardboard. Rocco is a popular saint and must allow himself to be treated familiarly. Not Jerome. ("Pray to St Jerome?" a young girl said to me the other day. "Who would ever dare? It's the same as with St Augustine: they are both so learned!") San Rocco is very much a neighborhood church frequented by the local people. In St Jerome, on the contrary, we can enjoy an aristocratic solitude, a pleasant tranquillity, seated on one of the high-backed, well-polished heavy wooden benches, quietly reviewing memories of our peregrinations through the Hieronymian City.

1. "Devotee" or "keeper of this spiritual library."

VIII

A VISION of ceremonies and of ecclesiastical ornamentations—the treatise "Of Priestly Vestments," *Letter LXIV,* addressed to Fabiola. We enter the Temple of Jerusalem where the Pontiff and the Levites array themselves, these predecessors of our clergy, since we are Israel. Jerome describes one by one these sacred habits, their shapes, their colors, the detail of the embroidery and of the ornaments, and he tells us what these things mean. The four elements, the planets, the names of the tribes, the seventy-two little bells sewn down the sides of the tunic called Meil and which resound when the Pontiff goes into the Sanctum sanctorum. The figure thus covered with cosmic symbols seems raised above mankind, the intermediary between a fallen Adam and God. This is why he must not set foot outside the sanctuary, nor move far away from the sacred objects, nor have any commerce with the unholy. "How many monks have lost their souls for having yielded to compassion for their father and mother! We are not allowed to sully ourselves through affection for [*super:* because of] our parents; and how much more carefully must we eschew feelings of attachment for our brothers, sisters, cousins and servants. We are of royal and priestly line. Let us wholly devote ourselves to that Father who never dies, or dies for us. . . ." No leaving the sanctuary. No hobnobbing with the local people; toward all earthly things, detachment; for we are of royal and sacred lineage. . . . How close this whole commentary on Leviticus seems to Plotinus' teaching: "Be not satisfied with the here and now" and "Flee, thou who art alone, unto him who is alone"; how close to the last chapter of the last *Ennead!* Elsewhere in Jerome's works we find the Bishop and the King compared; thus, he advises a future bishop to be more like a priest than a sovereign: "If it does not become a King to give way to pity and tears," he writes, "how much more unfitting are these in a Bishop. . . ." That is how cardinals (the *other* cardinals) will one day humbly request, and accept as a concession made to the temporal powers, the *tratamiento,* the prerogatives and the honors bestowed upon Royal Highnesses; and thus did it come to pass that Peter harbored in the shadow of his throne and keep for the convenience of the peoples, a college of seventy Kings. . . . The Pontiff and the Levites, under their raiments bearing the colors of the Universe, are Kings whose realm is nowhere to be seen except upon these raiments themselves; and even more than Kings, because to uniqueness their hieratic quality adds the incommensurable. How far we are, all of a sudden, from Athens: squarely in the midst of an oriental monarchy, in the world of secret lores and sealed books to whose threshold Herodotus had timidly led us. But of all the cults, the one whereof Jerome speaks was the most secret and the purest. He who is the subject of that cult defined Himself through the absolute notion of Being, and refused to be ranked alongside other gods. He was to offend Rome by his refusal to take a place in the pantheons. For he wanted Rome to be his alone for all eternity. He was the guest who stops on the doorstep. And when finally he enters—Ulysses among the Suitors—it is to announce that he is the sole legitimate master there. The wedding; the conclusion of the long engagement between East and West; the mediator, Greece; and Rome, the wedded pair's abode.

Naturally, there were those (among others, Lactantius, I believe) who said that Plato had plagiarized the Scriptures, and later—in our day—some people will say that St Paul must be included among the neo-Platonists and that his orthodox interpreters were inspired by Plotinus. But if that is as true as the claim that Plotinus proceeds from Plato, we have come full circle, and everything returns to the Synagogue: *"Et de sanctis non egredietur"* (Lev. XXI:12).

Was Jerome, who is so curious about Levitical tradition, so strongly attached to the 'Hebraic Truth,' so suspicious of the Seventy, and always in secret contact with the Synagogue—in Rome, Jerome regularly borrowed books from the Jews; in the desert, his Jew, Baranina, was always by his side—; was Jerome clearly aware of this transfer of Eastern thought into Western thought, and of the fusion, as it appears to us today, of these two traditions within Catholic orthodoxy? Perhaps. He so much wanted it. He so much contributed to it. But he speaks from above, beyond the years and the centuries; and while we listen to him as he holds forth on "The Priestly Vestment," we see, rising above the Synagogue where we were, the Cathedral where we were to be.

I X

JEROME'S own contradictions about his Dream ("You lie, you are not a Christian, but a Ciceronian") can be explained, even better than by his tendency to hyperbole and as a reaction of his critical mind, by the fact that the period when the dream occurred (and he certainly did not invent it) was precisely when he began his exegetic labors. He remorsefully considered all the time he devoted to reading the pagan authors as time taken away from penitence and the reading of the Scriptures. Aggravated by fever and illness, this feeling of guilt produced the grandiose nightmare of which, upon awakening, he retained so vivid a memory that he was later able to speak of it as of a vision, and that he thought very seriously, while convalescing, of honoring his vow not to have any further commerce with profane authors. But later still, when he had behind him years of scriptural study, and he was able to read the Old Testament not only in Greek but in Hebrew and in Syriac as well, he went back to the principles of his early education: the "humanities" are of undeniable usefulness, and are even indispensable to the mind's development. The *Letter to Magnus* (*Letter LXX*) is a clear statement of his point of view and shows that a literature altogether free of tradition was to him as inconceivable as a literature unrelated to any language. Moreover, he cites in his favor the example of the Christian authors of the two preceding centuries, as well as that of St Paul, and even of some authors of the Old Testament who referred to pagan writers.

And here we glimpse the course of Jerome's intellectual development. During his student years, the Latin Sirens (who, apparently, were better at their job than most of ours) succeeded in winning him to the love of Literature as exemplified in authors of the Republican and Octavian periods. He acquired a taste and a knack for the well-turned sentence, for the well-born (*generous*) phrase, slowly and delicately drawn from the depths of his thought, and felicitous, aglow from careful modeling. And true it is that despite his massive philological erudition, his religious ardor, his polemic fury, and his prejudices, he has the power and the ability to express with grace and serenity the product of his vigorous and fertile mind; and, as in Vasari's painting,[1] Venus and the cupids nearly adjoin him, even if he turns his back on them. He has that faculty—the rarest—of writing deeply into our memory. Expressed by someone else, the same thought does not hold, but fades away like the memory of a child that died in the cradle, or like water splashed on a plaster wall. Written by Sallust or by Montesquieu, by Sir Thomas Browne, Flaubert, or Jerome, it penetrates, remains, and expands in us. Was it not, then, the same thought? But here we find ourselves awfully close to the question of the unity of the intellect. Let us proceed.

And so, as soon as he finished studying in Rome, he must have known he was going to be a writer, and prepared himself for it. Then

1. A *Temptation of St Jerome*, now located in Florence's Pitti Palace. (Tr. note.)

Jesus—neglected (despite Jerome's Catholic background), forgotten in the course of "the disorders of his youth"—appeared. The visits to the Catacombs; baptism; the journey to Trier where he began to read the Latin exegetes and in addition to his pagan authors to collect a library of Christian Latin books. The religious calling becomes ever more insistent, but it is bound up with the literary vocation. As soon as he can read Greek fluently, Jerome discovers the greatest treasures of Christian literature, in particular Origen, who becomes, in his eyes, the human master *par excellence*. From then on, for him, Christian literature eclipses the pagan, and there is no writer more partisan than he to the Moderns, and more hostile to the Ancients.

It seems difficult for us to recapture the viewpoint from which the Church Fathers judged each other across one or two centuries. Yet the laws ruling intellectual history were the same then as today: generations of minds, both enriching and enriched, giving and receiving; the filiation between masters and disciples, the disciples being of two kinds: a small number capable of engendering and of becoming in their turn the masters of one or several succeeding generations; and a large number of "neuters" whose work remains sterile, whose thinking does not beget anything, and the whole crowd of imitators, of vulgarizers and of plagiarists who pass on the seed such as they received it, but unenriched, or who serve to carry it unconsciously, the way hornets transport the pollen of a few plants and birds broadcast seeds (as if through a precaution of Nature: insurance in case some seminal works were to disappear?). Thus, Origen must have been for Jerome simply what Victor Hugo or Tristan Corbière or Mallarmé or Dostoievski or Walt Whitman have been for some of us, and what Tertullian had been for Cyprian. But what is peculiar to Jerome's case and probably to that of most of the Christian writers of the early centuries, is that although he senses and recognizes within himself other influences—non-Christian ones—and sees the linkage which, from generation to generation, connects him to pagan art and thought, he is above all attentive to the Judaic and Evangelical current whose mighty force bears him along as in his view it bears along and revitalizes everything else. The Bible becomes an as yet little known world that needs to be explored, whose map must be drawn. And so it is he would give away all pagan literature and all of Plato—*stultus Plato*—for just one of the five or six thousand treatises or homilies of Origen, a very shrewd explorer of that unknown world; and he would do it only the more willingly since he rediscovers in Origen elements of Greek philosophy which he had known and loved, thanks to Cicero and Seneca, Virgil and Lucan. And how could Origen not be preferable, superior to Plato, even though Plato, by recommending as the basis of philosophy the unceasing meditation upon death, soared above all other pagan thinkers? Origen is a Christian; he possesses the Truth that Plato could only dimly make out, and he knows that *aliud est vivere moriturum, aliud mori victurum.*[1]

X

MEN of little or no faith at all, if we proceed to ponder those words, and if—as with Jerome himself whenever, tirelessly, pitilessly, triumphantly, he resumes his great theme of Virginity—we run up against the madness (in Latin, the "foolishness") of the Cross, what will be our response? Probably to recall the words, so solemn, so sad and so religious, which Symmachus puts in the mouth of hoary old Rome entreating their Eternities the Emperors to restore the Victory altar: "One does not immediately attain, at a sin-

1. "It is one thing to live with death in mind, quite another to die with the idea of living." (Tr. note.)

gle try, something [the Truth] so well hidden." (*Uno itinere non potest perveneri ad tam grande secretum.*[1]) And the fact that Rome is still young, adolescent under its beautiful black tresses (the holm oaks between the sky and us), and St Ambrose's reply "What you do not know, we have learned from God's very lips" (*Quod vos ignoratis id nos Dei voce cognovimus*)—will these be enough to fan into a fire that poor little spark of faith that we may perhaps carry within us? We know, we practice, as writers, the unceasing meditation on death, and even we know—or we hope—that (in a certain sense) we shall die in order to live; and we often descend unto those regions of "the empty skull and unending laughter" (Paul Valéry) where Shakespeare and Cervantes, Tolstoy and Balzac, Jerome and Augustine meet; and that, we know, is the ground where the most durable works of art are built. But will we ever venture into that metaphysical land, all the way to the mysterious spot where

> *. . . tenuis qua semita monstrat*
> *ire per angustam regna caelestia portam?*[2]

We too see the advantages of chastity, and know its price. As young men, we were all able to measure the amount of time that the grossest and most common pleasures stole from our most subtle and most personal ecstasies, and we know that scientific research, study, and art are demanding wives, and that when energy and radiance infuse works of the spirit these are almost always obtained—whether we like it or not—at the expense of the pleasures of the flesh. And it is still another noteworthy fact that this special sensitivity which lies at the basis of all

---

1. Gaston Boissier (*La fin du Paganisme*) translates as follows: "One path alone cannot be enough to arrive at such a great mystery."
2. ". . . the Celestial Realm one attains by a small path and through a narrow gate." (Tr. note.)

artistic (and perhaps scientific) creativity is born and develops within the individual before the age of puberty; as if the gift of poetry were reserved for virgins, and that is perhaps the meaning of the myth of the Muses. We would therefore be strongly inclined to reiterate with Jerome that marriage is silver, and virginity gold; and we think, as does he, that physical paternity, when compared with intellectual or spiritual paternity, is in no way desirable. We admire as a work of art his doctrine concerning Perpetual Virginity and "the brothers and sisters of Jesus," and even if Christianity is for us but another mythology, we cannot imagine the Universal Church prostrate at the feet of some fertile mother. Jerome: precursor of Dante, herald of Beatrice, the father of all literature of chivalry! He is also the moralist who, through his advocacy of virginity and vows of chastity, did the most to free the individual from family ties and women from male domination, placing them on the same plane as men ("In Christ's service, there are no differences of sex, only of spirit"). But when from there he goes on to try to convince us that only martyrdom can thoroughly cleanse us of "the filth [or the turpitude] of marriage" (*sordes nuptiarum*). . . .[1] Here, the spirit or rather the demon of contradiction whispers in our ear Thomas Middleton's line:

What a delicious breath marriage sends forth . . .

And as far as renunciation of the world is concerned, clearly it is in that direction the spirit is drawn in order to create its niche outside of, apart from a life of routine, from the pursuit of ambition and worldly

1. It is through this type of statement and because of the chastity vows he recommended to the newly-married couple that Jerome has given the impression he derided marriage, just as the legendary St Anthony mocks earthly courage and honor. But statistics and simple, everyday experience refute the objections of a few theologians: how many male virgins? How many abstinent young couples? How many men capable of turning the other cheek?

well-being. In the direction of a sit-down in favor of inaction and of "the flight of him who is alone towards him who is alone." But then. . . . And again for the man of little or no faith at all, Symmachus' words come to mind.

X I

VERY quickly, one begins to detect and recognize the inflections of Jerome's voice, the pace of his thought, his style. The pace of the sentence, even when it is short (its resonance); its quiver, its crackle: the sudden burst of an *Episcopi!* at the beginning of a period; the *capita columnarum* in the famous passage depicting Jesus dying of hunger on our doorstep, disguised as a pauper. And the art of the well-chosen detail: St Paula's last words uttered *in Greek* (she, the Roman lady, so totally estranged that she forgets her native tongue, even at that supreme moment). And we note also that he almost totally avoids the charge that has been levelled at the Church Fathers, including St Augustine, of allowing pulpit oratory to ruin his style. (Jerome's sermons and oral commentaries, published by Dom Morin, show that he was not a "great preacher.") He has neither the depths nor the flights of Augustine's eloquence, although Jerome too had "an uneasy adolescence" and often writes in the first person about private matters: there is much "self-display" even in the exegetical treatises; but he is more reserved, more distant, and never indulges in the confidential and tremulous "lyricism" that tires us, at times, in St Augustine. The over-abundance of diminutives and of the poetic plural (e.g., *tua colla*[1]) bothers somewhat, though these probably are conces-

1. Literally: "your necks" (when speaking to one person), seemingly a fashionable conceit at the time. (Tr. note.)

sions to the literary fashion of his day. But he has a fluidity and despite his powerfulness an aerial agility and a graphic precision that compel our admiration. They explain why we stay with him even in the *Letters,* the *Prefaces* and the *Homilies,* laden with erudite discussions, and in themselves devoid of general human interest—for example, the *Letter* (**XX**) to Pope Damasus "On the word Hosanna." He shows us what he sees, interests us in what fascinates him: particular customs, geographical and ethnic observations, linguistic and historical ideas. Rather than biographies, the *Life of Malchus* and of *Paul the Hermit* are poems of the Desert which they render in somewhat the same "visionary" manner as *The Rhyme of the Ancient Mariner* and the *Bateau ivre* render the Sea. The appearance of the Hippocentaur, the latter's conversation with St Anthony, and its disappearance, constitute one of those poetic miracles that come about two or three times in a century. Most of the descriptions of landscapes, of animals (the ants, the camels in *Malchus*) are of a truly magical clarity. And there is the exquisite end to the *Life of St Hilarion* in the small garden on the island of Cyprus where, although the body of the saint was no longer there (it had been carried back to his homeland) many miracles occurred, "perhaps because he was so fond of it." (A salute to the love of one's country!) And the *Letter to Gaudentius* (**XXVIII**) on the subject of the education of the little girl Pacatula (which also contains some sharp attacks against certain churchly persons, monks and bigots), with its lovely vignettes of youth: the "enclosed Danae" and the passage: "But when the uneducated and toothless little virgin"—*edentulam:* the little toothless one—"reaches the age of seven and starts to blush and to know what she must not say, and to hesitate about what she must say. . . ." It is a pity we cannot reread, right here, sheltered from outdoor distractions, some of the pages just come to mind; a pity we do not have here, at our disposal (of their own accord, our eyes probe the dim light of the chapels) the large and beautiful volumes of the Vallarsi edition where we could take up again our exploration of the Hieronymian City, and, making our way back across the main squares and districts we know fairly well, head for the broad avenues that open up on the other side: those commentaries on the Scriptures where we are sure to find many more of the things we love: erudition without pedantry, experience, literary criticism, and especially those beautiful, luminous, angelic poetic constructions whose charm, like the finest music, carries away our soul. . . . Or else we might perhaps reread the *Letter* (LVII) to Pammachius on "The Best Way to Translate," that *De Optimo Genere Interpretandi* which should be our breviary. . . . But no doubt books are useless where the Church tells us Truth and Life reside, and where that little light on the altar reminds us that "They are here. . . ." Yet, one could well imagine, next to Jerome's abode, a library entirely given over to his works, to his commentators and biographers, and, logically, to translations of the Bible. And the more so in as much as, not very far from here, young Augustine (*aetate filius, dignitate parens*[1]) owns, under the same roof that shelters his church, one of the famous libraries of this continent, his and that of the Augustinians, and which has, of all libraries, the loveliest name: the Angelic. . . . Here where we are, ye men of much reading and of very little faith, you will only find God and the memory of his translator. . . . The sound of footsteps, a jingling of keys, and a voice, a "Si chiude"[2] which rings like the *Finis* of the libraries; and outside, the Roman twilight.

Jerome's house, solitary on its street corner, close to the river and to the river bank he may have had in mind when he talked about navigation and the arrival in port of the "divine merchandise" he sent from the Greek to the Latin world; a simple house, a facade which from a

1. "A son in terms of age, a father in terms of rank." (Tr. note.)
2. "Closing time!" (Tr. note.)

distance resembles a silver plaque, a finely-chiseled cartouche; bearing the brilliant coats-of-arms—upon three boxes painted in extra-fine colors—of a Pope, of a Cardinal, and of the King of Serbia; a house paved with Dalmatian marble, perhaps legally situated on Yugoslav territory, and in this too very Roman, very cosmopolitan; the house of the Translator, resting in the peaceful coolness come from the river, at the end of a final curve in the street. "O happy rooftops," O happy, seldom-visited house, remote and isolated in the heart of the city like some nobleman's home, you remind us of the magnificent opening of a sentence from Villemain which we found in the article on "Jerome (Saint)" in a French and agnostic encyclopedia: "Kept at a distance from ecclesiastical honors, always on the move or solitary, without any title in the Church but that of priest of Jesus Christ. . ."

X I I

A MISLEADING statement. What one author has called "the travels of St Jerome," when examined chronologically, appears instead as a series of residences, each lasting several years, in six or seven of the West and East's principal cities, and in Bethlehem, in the midst of his spiritual family and of his monks. Receiving visitors and pilgrims from all parts not only of the Empire but of the entire known world, one cannot say that Jerome was "solitary."

That same sentence ends, less splendidly than it began, with these words: ". . . he did not appear at the court nor at the funeral of any prince. He was not assigned the task of teaching or consoling the people of any great city. . . ." Villemain must have been thinking of St Ambrose or St Augustine; but his picture of the life of Jerome seems to us tainted by bourgeois preconceptions—French nineteenth century bourgeois. His Jerome is an oddity, almost a failure; he did not follow the approved path; he ought to have shown more drive, more ambition, more flexibility towards his enemies, taken advantage of his connections and of the reputation he had acquired, in order to rise in the hierarchy and become bishop of one of the imperial cities and of Rome itself; he owed this to himself, to us: a social success proportionate to his intellectual greatness; and we should be able to find his name on the list of the Popes as we find it on that of the Fathers of the Latin Church of the fourth century. Yes, just as we should encounter Seneca's name on the list of the Emperors! As a matter of fact, this almost came to pass, in both cases; but are Seneca and Jerome diminished in any way, the former for not having succeeded Nero, and the latter, Pope Damasus? But this whole discussion about Jerome's "career" is pointless. It is enough to consider that he was a monk, and one of the masters, if not the master, of the monasticism of his day. He was located on a plane which was not that of the secular clergy, and in a sphere of religious life from which titles and honors were excluded out of principle. One may argue that Bishop John of Jerusalem was also a monk; but he and Jerome, as head of an important monastic community, dealt with each other as equals. One must also consider his reputation as a writer and exegetist, indeed very much questioned and often very harshly treated by his critics, but without any doubt famous from the days of his "cardinalate" on, and illustrious in his Bethlehem retreat. But the author of the passage in question, who manifestly was thinking of official honors only (though they frequently are no sure sign of any power, even temporal) took no account of Jerome's effective intellectual influence.

IN REALITY, Jerome enjoyed literary fame during all of the second half of his existence; and his posthumous life in the minds of men, down to Raphael, to Correggio and Domenichino, continues and culminates his physical life instead of transfiguring it. Let us betake ourselves to those wonderful windows that give out upon limitless mornings, let us step inside those painted dreams. After the sun has set upon a certain 30th of September some fifteen hundred years ago, after the jostle, the heat and the dust of his mortal day, the writer returns to the serenity of his works and rests there, contented, till the end of time. The Jerome of the painters, whom we find throughout Europe, from Naples to Paris and London, from Stockholm to Vienna and Madrid, is not a legendary figure, some mythical monk glorified by the peoples' devotion in ignorant and barbarous times, but the man of letters he really was—some of the desert backgrounds even seem to be inspired by his own descriptions—and we are neither surprised nor shocked to see him now at the top of some Christian Mount Olympus, suggestive of the world his mind inhabited, now in Dante's company; and, within that pictorial biography, everywhere associated with what we call "the spirit of the Renaissance," just as, geographically, the Spanish saw him linked to the colonization of the New World. The *Temptations,* the *Dreams,* the *Penitences* are so many illustrations of *Letter XXII.* Correggio's *Day* is not an arbitrary composition, an extravaganza, a pretext for effects of light and glorious female flesh tints, and without any connection with the historical Jerome; nor is it the representation of a vision, but a kind of biographical synthesis, a summation of the life, the meditations and the literary works of the Saint in Bethlehem. It is even likely that when he painted that picture, Allegri[1] had in mind *Letter XLIV, De Sanctis Locis,* written to Marcella under the names of Paula and Eustochium, and the passage in this *Letter* where he describes the *Villula Christi.*[2] The setting is the cave where the Manger is; the action, "that which is better honored by silence than by clumsy words." Jesus, seated on Mary's lap, represents Bethlehem-Ephrata; Magdalene, at Mary's feet, symbolizes the Penitence in the desert; she is the celestial friend of the cloistered nuns of Paula and Eustochium's convent; the book being presented to Jesus is, of course, the Vulgate, and, in the right-hand corner, the Translator stands in person. In the *Dispute of the Holy Sacrament,* it is apparent that Raphael was thinking of the often quoted sentence by Sulpicius Severus about Jerome. Truly, few of the great painters have found their Hieronymian subjects elsewhere than in Jerome's own works or those of his more reliable contemporaries; and if they have not taken into account those passages which give us a few indications of our writer's physical aspect—thus, for example, the anecdote about the bronze sphere used by Athenian athletes and placed near Minerva's statue; the "frail body which, even when he is in good health, remains weak"; and his frequent illnesses—, it is because they could not do otherwise, and, choosing as models tall and powerful old men, they transposed his moral qualities into physical ones. And it is clear that the attributes borrowed from the Legendary Lives[3] have, for them as for us, a purely symbolic value.

Besides, the subjects extracted from these legends are not entirely alien to Jerome the writer. Indeed, the *Medieval Lives*[3] where Jerome is depicted are the work of people who, though ignorant and credulous, admire him and attempt, with more or less success, to imitate his style

1. Correggio's actual family name. (Tr. note.)
2. "Jesus' cottage." (Tr. note.)
3. References to *The Golden Legend* and other Lives of the Saints. (Tr. note.)

and adopt his manner. Thus, one of them—who was immediately copied by another—must have particularly enjoyed Jerome's animal descriptions. We are referring to the author who relates the whole absurd
legend of the Lion and who assures us that *"Tribus claudicans, quarto
suspensus pede, ingens leo coenobii claustra ingressus est."*[1] The rhythm is
there. But where are the delicate touch and the polish of the Master?

X I V

A CRUCIFIX, a lion, a stone, a skull

and ". . . the materials needed for writing." Surely, seeing so many St
Jeromes which show an old man reading or composing a book, a person who knew nothing about the history of Christianity would grasp
that Jerome was above all a writer, and, after having been told what a
saint is for a Christian, and about all the lovely mytho-hagiography that
enters into the daily lives of the people of the old Catholic countries—
St Lawrence, patron saint of archivists, St Lucy, protectress of eyesight,
etc.—he would be tempted to see in Jerome the patron saint not only
of translators, but of all men of letters.

1. "Limping on three feet, the fourth one uplifted, a huge lion entered the hermits'
cloister." (Tr. note.)

HE would also see that the Graces almost always accompany him, all through his painted biography, and that even in the desert he is in the company of "choirs of angels." They surround him, watch over him, lean over his books, turn for him the pages of the 'Hebraic Truth,' serve him as dictionaries, all adorable figures that a pagan would mistake for winged nymphs or for Aurora, or Hebe, or Ganymede. Above the clouds supported by youthful Glories, in mid-air on Parma's church ceilings, some one of these adolescent nudities is always near him; and till the hour of his death Beauty is there: the figure, Youth itself, kneeling on the right in the Communion.[1]

And in this illuminated commentary on St Jerome it does not seem inappropriate to find, now and then, the Roman purple—upon two occasions, mantling his shoulders. Rather than an anachronism, it strikes us as a sort of posthumous promotion. And what a wonderful and arresting sight, when his painters place him in the desert and in the traditional poses of Penitence and . . . of Translation, clad in the full regalia of a Priest-Cardinal of the Holy Roman Church. O King of the endless sand's blonde waves, and of the rocks eaten away by the lion of the Zodiac and by baying Anubis! That hat and that purple which would command such respect and so many honors in Rome and at the court of the most potent monarchs, he wears them in a dreadful landscape, itself an accumulation of misshapen solitudes that bear almost no relation to the Earth—witness the sundered rock and the stunted tree behind him in the Stockholm canvas.[2] Provided our imagination

1. Probably an allusion to Botticelli's *The Last Communion of St Jerome.* (Tr. note.)
2. By the seventeenth century French painter Georges de La Tour. (Tr. note.)

can accept the theme of the painting, the impact is strong. To be sure, one's memory and good sense quickly correct that impression, remind us of that unfortunate overlay of monastic legends which for so long (down to Erasmus' Preface, according to Ferdinand Cavallera[1]) distorted Jerome's biographies; and we cannot help but say to ourselves that the tailor and the hatter must not be far. But that Cardinal in the borderlands between Earth and Sky is also the author of the Vulgate. And who knows whether from out of his purple robe he couldn't provide us with the live coals to heap on our enemy's head, were we perchance to consider that sumptuous and useless vestment as a symbol of our smugness and vanity, of our need of praise and of all the sham glory we feast on indefatigably? "Detach yourselves from the world's good opinion of you," he would enjoin us; "flee from your own success; say to yourself that the generation for which you are writing, painting, or composing music is not yet born—and that perhaps time will end before it even has a chance to be born. Do not look for any satisfaction outside of your work, which alone is worthy of your care, and alone must count for you since that work *is* you. For its sake, rid yourself of all ties. That way, and in the midst of your obscurity and solitude, you will, upon occasion, just as you place the final period, hear that angels' applause." And he might add: ". . . and in your hours of discouragement and of doubt, or of remorse, in order to regain confidence in yourself or to atone for some sin committed against your demanding Muse, get back humbly into the traces and humbly translate; in a spirit of charity and of justice, and for the glory of one of your brothers, translate. . . ."

But in reality it is a totally different exhortation, or rather a song of triumph, that Jerome's purple robe calls to mind. The posthumous promotion has had a double, retroactive effect, for it is Jerome in the

1. F. Cavallera, *Saint Jérôme, sa vie et son oeuvre,* Champion Editeur (1922).

desert of Chalcis[1] that we have in front of us, Jerome before his pseudo-cardinalate; and it is the final "canto" of his *Exhortation to Heliodorus* (*Letter XIV*) that he sings to us: *"O desertum Christi floribus vernans . . .":* "O desert ablaze with Christ's flowers! O solitude where these stones are born, whereof is built, in the Apocalypse, the city of the Great King! Believe me, I see here I know not what beyond the light. . . . What are you doing in this world, my brother, you who are beyond its measure?"

This is no flattery: for Jerome, every Christian is "too great for this world" since "we have been redeemed at so great a price." Here, in this *celeuma epilogi*—this final song—, the mad passion for the Cross bursts with irresistible poetic force, and exults with the evocation of the Last Judgment amidst the sounding of the Trumpet and the "howling of the Universe," when "Plato the imbecile" and "Aristotle the quibbler" are confounded, along with "Jupiter aflame,"[2] before the throne of the "Son of the worker and of the mercenary."[3] Of course all these words have their sources in St Paul (in the Apocalypse), in St John Crysostom, and in Tertullian; but Virgil (and he too has his sources) never rose to such heights of sublime delirium, denying all human wisdom, destroying every city, annihilating the earth, and hurling man into the heavens.

1. The Syrian desert, near Aleppo. (Tr. note.)
2. Ignitus Jupiter. Probably a poetic way of referring to the Stoics.
3. According to Apocryphal tradition, the Virgin Mary worked in her home as a spinner. (Tr. note.)

YET, we must not be so dazzled by a splendid passage as to adopt the opinion of those prejudiced or indoctrinated critics who are ready to follow Jerome with respect to Origen and Plato and who will declare, for instance, that St Ambrose's *De Officiis* "is just as superior to Cicero's as Christian wisdom is superior to Greek and Roman philosophy." Cicero and Ambrose are one thing, "Christian wisdom" another. Actually, through the use of cleverly selected quotations, it would be easy to show, on the one hand, that the best Church Fathers are more profound, more humane writers, etc., than the greatest pagan authors; or on the other, to show that the advent of Christian thought within Latin literature resulted in an overall lowering of the intellectual, aesthetic, and even moral quality of the works produced. The two opinions are equally wrong, as is the theory, in part Hieronymian, of equivalences: Eusebius = Herodotus, Lactantius = Cicero, Sulpicius Severus = Sallust, and so on. One should, instead, consider these writers individually; bear in mind to what degree of sterility Latin literature had sunk by the time the first Christian writers appeared upon the scene; lay aside, once and for all, the childish notion of "good Latinity"; and above all take into account the essential factor of time, for it is only with Dante that Christian literature produced a poet comparable to Virgil. It seems to us that, in general, one is rather unfair toward Christian writers of the third through the fifth centuries, and that connoisseurs should recognize without quibbling that a poet like Prudentius is as worthy to be read, studied and cherished, as Propertius or Tibullus. Prudentius, the ancestor of Spanish lyric poetry, the one voice in all of Romania that brings us a little closer to the lost paradise of Latin lyric poetry.

As regards Jerome, it must be acknowledged, his mad passion for the Cross did not always inspire him as beautifully as in *Letter XIV*. He drags, at times, and repeats himself; and his commentary on the Beatitudes is disappointing. The incomplete homily that represents Jerome in the "Roman Breviary," under the date of the 30th September, is typical as a mixture of pure and simple paraphrase, quotations, and strong Hieronymic style. But this strength lessens through the excessive use of paraphrase and quotations, and in the systematic search for Biblical concordances. It is true that part of his art consists in blending the Latin and Judaic literary traditions, and this he manages fairly well: the great English and French sermonists and the Romantics have seldom done better, and Lammenais much less well. But often, however, the various borrowed elements, both sacred and profane, have been left intact, as quotations, with or without references; the assembled material has not been worked over, and some passages are so crammed with literary allusions that they resemble centoes,[1] and one is led to wonder whether, during certain periods of low culture, people have not quoted Sallust, Cicero and Persius, imagining they were quoting Jerome. And of course there is the polemical part, so intrusive and, for us, so thoroughly dead: the "clodhoppers," the "barking dogs," the "Spanish vipers" (from Iberia, needless to say) and the "scorpions," the occasional "son of an innkeeper" and "pig-head" and the long story of the quarrel over Origen, which ends up with Jerome's hurrahs upon learning of Rufinus' death.

What he says about slander, "a mere flash in the pan," applies also to polemics as a literary form. It is of interest to contemporaries only, that is, those contemporaries with time to waste, those bubble-heads who concern themselves a lot, and uselessly, with other people; the gossips

1. Patchwork pieces of writing, prose or verse. (Tr. note.)

and the mediocrities whose very envy is weak-livered and who enjoy watching people in the forefront insult, ridicule and revile each other. These disputes, which took on so much importance in Jerome's life and which, added to his desire for independence, successively drove him away from Aquileia, Antioch and Rome, became, with time, fame and "canonization," the Holy Doctor's "tribulations." All of his enemies were eventually condemned without appeal, and without any exception have become "the enemies of orthodoxy." "The reader may be astonished that such holy figures could have had enemies. But this is not surprising: envy always besets the meritorious." Thus did one of his medieval panegyrists express himself, in whose eyes he was the first among the Doctors of the Church, whose writings "shine all across the world like divine lamps" and "like unto the sun, bathe all in light, from East to West." He visited every country, knew every language, lived over one hundred years; and, four hundred years after his death, some cardinal who in an assembly spoke ill of his writings, was seized by a deadly colic. "One does not malign men of worth with impunity."

Reading Jerome, however, one easily understands that his stubborn and contentious disposition, his extremely touchy pride where his writings were involved, and his fiery temperament, must have played a part in his "tribulations," and that he often reaped what he had sown. He exposed himself to his jealous detractors, provoking them by his diatribes, his verbal excesses, his scoffing. To be sure, he fled and went into seclusion (... *fugientem me et inclusum*); he even vowed to hold his peace, so as not to vex his enemies. One wishes he had kept his promise, but on the contrary, he shouted louder, better, and longer than any of them. And since he possessed the art of writing works that endure, while his opponents were intellectual "neuters" whose productions have sunk into oblivion, the result is that he seems always to have fought with adversaries who were no match for him: all that anger, all that roaring appear directed at scarecrows and manikins. In point of fact, they were formidable celebrities, some of them treacherous and unprincipled, and who had disinterested supporters. Rufinus, for instance, was, in the view of his contemporaries, comparable to Jerome as a writer; it was in his translation that Christians all over the West had read Eusebius' *Ecclesiastical History,* and that we still read the terrifying tale of the torturing of Christians in Lyon. Observing this contest, the public could suspect either one of being jealous of the other, and in the theological dispute see the result of a rivalry between two men-of-letters. Posterity did not do justice to Rufinus who had the merit of abandoning this unseemly dispute and of no longer answering Jerome's insults, which had become rather ridiculous. (Such is the opinion, on this matter, of Jerome's most recent biographer, Ferdinand Cavallera.[1]) Ought we not then speak, instead, of "the tribulations of Rufinus"? At any rate, when next we enter a church dedicated to Jerome, let us have a thought for the other Translator, the one who lost, Rufinus of Aquileia; and let them thus be reconciled in men's memories, as they surely were in the Great Century.[2]

X V I I

LEAVING these Hieronymian precincts, once so animated—though it was not for long—and today so dull and lifeless, and continuing our journey away from the city's center, we enter the area which can be designated as that of "the naturalized aliens" or "the interlopers," the vast *Xenodochium*[3] in Jerome's

1. F. Cavallera, *Saint Jérôme,* tome II, p. 101.
2. I.e., the seventeenth, when Rufinus of Aquileia received much reverent attention from the Maurist Fathers (French Benedictines). (Tr. note.)
3. Reception center for foreigners. (Tr. note.)

works: his translations. Here are the *Chronicon* of Eusebius of Caesarea, several *Homilies* of Origen, a treatise of Didymus the Blind, Pachomius' *Rule*. . . . In fact, during all of his life, Jerome simultaneously composed original works and translated.

Very curious about the various idioms and dialects he heard spoken around him (in Gaul, in Asia Minor, etc.), he started translating as soon as he had a sufficient knowledge of Greek. In the beginning, "for the love of Greek"—and perhaps for sheer pleasure, as a philologist and a poet; and since he had studied it well enough to write it correctly, he indulged himself by completing in the original language the text he was working on—Eusebius' *Topics*—and then translating it from Greek into Latin.

It is probably Eusebius (or, possibly, St Hilarion) who led him to Origen's works, which he liked enormously: his translations of Origen stemmed from this warm admiration. A predilection of almost equal intensity for Didymus the Blind caused him to translate his *Treatise on the Holy Ghost*. In the preface to this translation, he writes: "I preferred to make my appearance as the translator of someone else's work rather than, ugly little blackbird that I am, adorning myself in someone else's brilliant colors." Here is the admission simultaneously of his admiration for the *De Spiritu Sanctu,* and of the temptation he felt of appropriating it, perhaps of copying or closely imitating it. And it is also the precise indication of the need, of the deep instinct that translating is a response to, and which makes, depending on the moral fiber or the degree of intelligence of the individual, either for plagiarists or for translators. Jerome was himself rich enough in knowledge and in ideas, and of strong enough mind, not to hesitate for long between vice and virtue, between plagiarizing and translating. Now one knows it is easier to copy than to translate, and Jerome had no illusion as to the difficulties of his task: "It is hard," he writes, "for him who follows another's

lines step by step, not to swerve away at any point, and to make sure
that what is well said in another language remains as beautiful [or
graceful: *eumdem decorem*] once translated." (*De Optimo Genere Interpretandi.*)

". . . *Quem ego in latinum verti. . . . Quem in latinum transtuli. . . .*"[1] he
writes in the last chapter of his *De Viris Illustribus,* where he catalogues
his own works. He translated out of love, that is because of his enthusi-
asm for certain works of his predecessors or of his exegetic masters. He
translated out of the desire to serve people, or to please his friends. He
translated in order to console himself for his disappointments, his great
sorrows: "*. . . aestuantis animi taedium interpretatione digerere conamur*"[2]
(after the Fall of Rome and the death of St Paula). He even translated
"against" people, that is, when he wanted to publicly denounce his adversaries' plagiarisms: "*Certe qui hoc legerit Latinorum juxta cognoscet,*"[3]
thus pressing his abilities as a translator into the service of his polemi-
cist's passions and grievances.

X V I I I

THE *De Optimo Genere Interpretandi*
can be considered the monumental gate through which one gains ac-
cess to Jerome's contribution as a translator. I have already said that it
ought to be our breviary, and to show that I practice what I preach, I
don't mind admitting here that in a moment of Hieronymian fervor I
copied it in its entirety from the Vallarsi edition, so that I own of this

1. "What I turn into Latin . . . What I translate into Latin. . . ." (Tr. note.)
2. "We attempt, through our translation work, to allay the weariness of our passionate
soul. . . ." (Tr. note.)
3. "No doubt, he who reads this [work or exposé on plagiarists] will recognize the pilfer-
ings of the Latin authors."

opus a unique copy. The work in question was written because of a particular episode in the quarrel over Origen—some private papers of Jerome's had been stolen and their content revealed—and one could wish he had devoted more space in it to the art of translation. There he sets forth his great principle: to render the meaning rather than the words of a text. Then, as is his wont, he introduces his references and looks for backers: Terence, Plautus, Cicero. The last two-thirds of the work consist in a demonstration of the fact that the Evangelists, like the Apostles, very freely translated the passages of the Old Testament that they cite, sometimes erring in their attributions, while the Seventy were often unfaithful to the 'Hebraic Truth.' Finally, he takes up his theme of the simplicity that is indispensable to the ecclesiastical style, ending with a fresh and thorough attack upon his enemies. As it stands, this *Letter LVII* contains the essential: the listing, complete with examples, of the greatest difficulties of the art of translation, and an ingenious illustration of the basic rule: *Non verbum e verbo, sed sensum exprimere de sensu,* a trick of the trade and a sort of *reductio ad absurdum:* "translate" a work in verse into prose, but within the same language. A few more passages from his works, such as the conclusion of *Letter XX* on "non-translatable" foreign words, which therefore must be borrowed, the rest of the preface to the *Chronicon* not cited in the *De Optimo Genere Interpretandi,* a few sentences from the *Prefaces* and which are given in most Latin editions of the Vulgate, etc. . . , complete this "Art of Translation."

HIERONYMOPOLIS is encircled by
two concentric lines of fortifications: one low, much damaged, almost
collapsed: Jerome's revision of the *Itala*,[1] one of the first Latin versions
of the Bible; the other tall, thick, powerful, awe-inspiring: the Vulgate.
Two high towers overlook these walls: the *Gallican Psalter* and the
Roman Psalter. It is generally through them, from without, that one
approaches Jerome's achievement: these towers and ramparts, visible
from afar, at the same time announce and hide the city. All the critics
and scholars who have studied Jerome have said that his "masterwork,"
his greatest title to glory, *laus praecipua*,[2] was the Vulgate. And this
opinion, often accepted with too much docility, is the reason why the
personal works of Jerome have been neglected in favor of his work as a
translator. "In conclusion, his most important work was the translation
of the Scriptures, an immense task rather than a work of genius," writes
the French author quoted above. An "immense task" *and* "a work of
genius" one ought rather to call it; and one should also define the
words "his most important work." The importance of the Vulgate has
no need of demonstration; it is one of our civilization's cornerstones,
and both St Peter's in Rome and New York's skyscrapers partly rest on
it. One might object that this role could have devolved on the *Itala*—
whether reviewed by Jerome or not—in the absence of his Vulgate. But
in that case, the Catholic Church would have a Book less faithful to the

---

1. According to modern specialists (A. D'Alès in his work on Novatius) one ought not
to say the *Itala* but the *Romana* or *Vetus Romana*. It is this version, made or received in
Rome in the third century, that Jerome calls *Vulgata*, the name subsequently given to his
own version.
2. A. Ficarra, preface to *Florilegium Hieronymianum*, published on the occasion of Jerome's
fifteenth centenary (1920).

original texts, and less well translated, of the great classics of Hebrew literature; one may also wonder whether such an anthology would have had the same success and the same influence (particularly from a linguistic standpoint) as Jerome's Vulgate. However, this so to speak practical or secondary importance of Jerome's "main work" must not prevent us from seeing the intrinsic value of his original work. There exists here a deliberate neglect, and its unfairness is of the same order as for example paying attention to Charles Baudelaire only insofar as he was the translator of Edgar Allan Poe. Whoever reads something of Jerome's own realizes at once that in the Vulgate he has before him a great book or rather a great body of literature translated by a great writer.

And that the Vulgate is truly a work of genius is confirmed by the qualities we discern there: that solidity, that grandeur, that majestic simplicity of style and expression. And the crumbs from this feast in which the Orient was served to the West have nourished and will continue to nourish generation upon generation of readers, writers, and poets to come. Would the *Itala* or *Vetus Romana* have been capable of doing the same? At any rate, it is in the wellsprings of Jerome's Vulgate that various literatures have found their inspiration, and, for our specific part, Bossuet, Racine and Claudel are all steeped in the vitalizing glow of those deep and living waters.

One must also take into account the prodigious inventive effort behind such a creation, and consider as well how the translator, having little by little, in his own works, got beyond the rules of rhetoric, the literary twists and conceits that he inherited from his masters, and forging constantly ahead—like Cervantes—toward greater freedom and simplicity, ended up by inventing a syntax, a style, an idiom, both popular and noble, that Latin—so different from the Latin of his *Letters*—which heralds the Romance languages, and which surely played a large role in their formation; or that "ecclesiastical interpretation which is intended," Jerome declares, "not for the prattling students of philosophers, nor for a few disciples, but for mankind as a whole" (*Letter XLIX*).

A greater effort, this, than the one needed to lift the bronze sphere in Athens! Particularly if one considers the distaste that Jerome had to overcome at the start of his exegetic career: a sort of horror when confronted by the language, the form, the novelty of Scriptural writing, whether he read the Septuagint or the Hebrew text. We too feel some of that surprise when we switch suddenly from the Greek classics to the Bible. Let us give it a try. Even if we have almost completely forgotten our Greek, let us take in the Septuagint a passage that is familiar to us thanks to various translations in one or several modern languages: a chapter from Job or Esther, or from the Song of Songs, for instance. We shall have little trouble understanding it; but how odd, we say to ourselves, for whom "Greek" is the Greek of Demosthenes or Thucydides. How strange, outlandish, scandalous this Greek is! Unheard-of constructions, juxtapositions serving in lieu of logical deductions, an endless phosphorescence of images, the magical and splendid desolation of some unknown ocean bottom: a new planet with its craters, its crevices, its valleys, suddenly visible to the naked eye, and with their earthen color that is not of this earth—the moon only a hundred yards away! Now we begin to have a faint idea of what Jerome must have felt when he was still imbued with Donatus' lessons and Cicero's and Quintillian's prose. But the day was to come when this strangeness would cease to shock him, and when he would see the beauty in this simplicity; the day when he would formulate his admirable and celebrated judgment of St Paul as a writer, a judgment worthy of Paul himself, and which concludes thus: *". . . sed quocumque respexeris, fulmina sunt."*[1]

1. ". . . but wherever you turn, there are flashes of lightning." (Tr. note.)

INDEED a Pontiff is he who gave
the Hebrew Bible to the West, and built the wide viaduct that joins
Jerusalem to Rome, and Rome to those nations where Romance
tongues are spoken or who have incorporated into their languages
Latin words and phrases which are, very often, those of the Vulgate,
Jerome's words and phrases, come into use with the most popular lines
of his Book. What other translator can be credited with a like achievement? What other translator has been able to bring off so colossal an
undertaking with so much success, and with consequences so far-reach-
ing in time and in space? For even the Authorized Version, despite all
the reworking and all the approximations to the Hebrew text, re-
joins—through Wycliffe—the Vulgate; and it is as if its deliberate ar-
chaism were a finery adopted in order to outdo, in minds dazzled by its
beauty, the deliberate modernism of Jerome. And thus he followed our
race across the sea, and his spirit is with us whither we have gone, and
words begot of his words praise the Lord to the sound of banjos where
Blacks sing spirituals and keen in the *tristes* and *modinhas* to the accom-
paniment of guitars in the distant lands where the dialect of Latium's
peasants fuses with the speech of Guarani Indians.

A great writer and an incomparable translator. But a translator, like
us. One who even made mistakes, like all of us; but who, like us, knew
the desire and the excitement, the sorrow and the joy, of translating;
and who knew the triumph of making intelligible for a whole people,
from generation to generation, that which for most of them was but
ink on paper. Why hold forth on "the eminent dignity of translators
within the republic of letters"? One need only utter the name of
Jerome, and the most humble among us immediately feels taller, and
reminded of the duties and the honor of his calling. Our very great,

most holy patron saint. On whose feast-day we should take the day off. Unless we choose that day—on the threshold of mellow October, season of study—to start a new translation.

So, before reopening our dictionaries and installing ourselves anew in our hallowed toil—in the toil, love, prudence and charity that are a translator's—we shall in our thoughts betake ourselves to Rome, and there we shall climb the Esquiline. The steps, all the steps to the Liberian basilica. And once we stand in the great house of Our Lady of the Snows, we shall move toward the *Presepio*.[1] St Jerome's chapel is on the right. And it is there that, on mentally bended knee, we shall ask him to sustain us in our labors.

Without flowery language. Without oratory. None of those Gallic theatrics. But with "Roman gravity" and the totally unadorned style of "the ecclesiastical interpretation." A short prayer that we shall attempt to compose for the use of our entire brotherhood.

It will start as does the prayer addressed to him by all Catholics on the 30th of September, a prayer one can find in the Common[2] of the Doctors: *O Doctor Optime. . .* , etc., and to it we shall add first of all the opening words of the last sentence in *Letter CXL: Aggrediar opus difficillimum. . .;* then, the end of his *Preface* to the Pentateuch: *Nunc te precor . . . ut me . . . orationibus tuis juves, quo possim eodem spiritu quo scripti sunt libri in Latinum transferre sermonem.* Of course, instead of "Latinum" we will use Gallicum or the name of whatever language we are translating into. Put into English the prayer will sound as follows: "Excellent Doctor, light of the Holy Church, blessed Jerome, I am about to embark upon a most difficult task, and ere I do I beseech you to aid me with your prayers, that I may translate this work into an English which preserves the same spirit it was composed in."

Thus, from the moment he is named till the final period, it contains

1. *Presepio:* the Manger. (Tr. note.)
2. Regular, recurring religious service. (Tr. note.)

not a word that is not his. We quote him as we speak to him. What author, no matter how accustomed to praise and glory, could, even in Paradise, receive with indifference such a compliment? He understands right away that these are exceptional clients who address him, suppliants who have acquired a very special right to his good will and protection. From Heaven on high, surrounded by his court of glossophile, grammarian and lexicographic angels, more beautiful even than Correggio's, and who work under his guidance on the never ending Dictionary of *all* the languages ever spoken or to be spoken by Adam's children, he is listening kindly; he nods his acceptance, and smiles: "And for the quotations, my thanks to you." In this life, and for all the ages to come, hail unto thee, O our heavenly friend.

The design of this book is the work of
Edmund Helminski, of Brattleboro, Vermont.
The typesetting has been by American–Stratford Graphic Services, Inc.,
also of Brattleboro, Vermont.
The printing and binding are by
McNaughton & Gunn, Inc., Ann Arbor, Michigan.